Dog Pound Buddy and the Twins

Written by
Jeanette Tomplait

Illustrations by Ramir Quintana

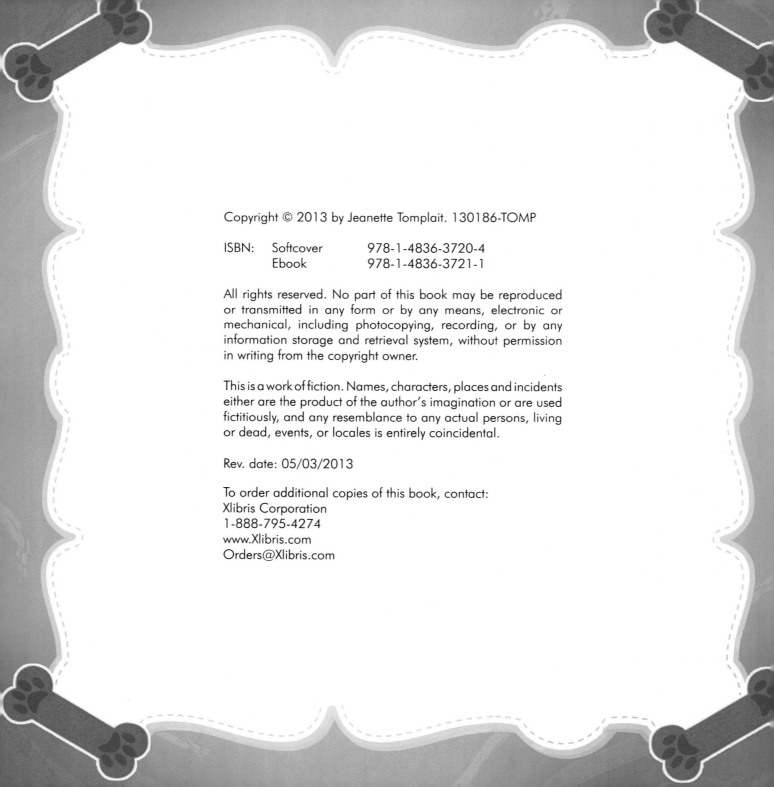

Rev. date: 05/03/2013

To order additional copies of this book, contact:
Xlibris Corporation
1-888-795-4274
www.Xlibris.com
Orders@Xlibris.com

TABLE OF CONTENTS

Buddy Gets His Dream Home

The tiny red miniature weenie dog sat staring through the gray wire fence with a sad look on his face. He had been brought to the dog pound by the dog catcher when he was found rummaging through some garbage on a nearby street. There was no sign of his mom, dad, or owner anywhere around. He was just a pup, about three or four weeks old, very scared and very hungry. As the dog catcher reached down to pick him up, the man said, "Come here, Buddy," and gently placed him into his coat pocket.

Each day, the dog catcher would pass by his pen and say "Hello, Buddy." Somehow that name, Buddy, stuck with him. Before long, all the caretakers were calling him Buddy.

Buddy did not like to be closed up in a cage, but he was so glad for the good food and the nice doghouse that the dog pound gave to him. But as the days went by, it seemed nobody wanted to adopt such a tiny red miniature weenie dog. He looked a lot like a hot dog without a bun. Many families with kids had come by the dog pound to pick out a pet, but they always pointed to him and laughed and then went on down to the other dog pens. Today seemed no different. The dog in the next pen had just left with his new family. He gave Buddy a farewell bark as they went by. Buddy barked back as if to say "Good luck! Wish it were me! Here goes another lonesome day!" Buddy's dream was to go home with a nice family with kids to play with.

Buddy started back inside his doghouse to take a nap and dream of his new home with a real family when, all at once, he heard loud voices coming down the walkway. He ran to the fence, and staring down at him was a little boy and a little girl dressed alike in blue overalls and red shirts shouting at the top of their lungs, "We want this puppy! Please, Mom and Dad, let us have this puppy for our birthday!"

Buddy thought for a minute that he must be dreaming. He had never seen a boy and girl that looked so much alike. He had never seen twins before, so he thought he was seeing double. As Mom and Dad came closer, he heard them say, "Kip and Kinzi, are you sure this is the puppy you want for your birthday? There are a lot of other puppies in the other cages." Buddy's heart seemed to stop as Mom, Dad, and the kids began walking toward the other pens. In an instant though, the two kids came running back, yelling, "We want this puppy! Please, please let us have this one!"

Buddy's heart started racing this time as he waited to see what his future would be. Could this be his new family? Would they really pick him as their pet? Would Mom and Dad say yes? This would be his dream come true!

Mom and Dad looked at each other and then back at the twins. With a shrug of their shoulders, they finally said, "Okay, Kip and Kinzi, we guess you can have this puppy for your birthday."

The twins were so excited that they began to jump up and down. They were turning three years old the next day, and they were promised a pet from the dog pound. Mom and Dad motioned to the caretaker to open up Buddy's pen and told him they wanted to take the tiny red miniature weenie dog home with them.

The twins' faces were beaming with delight as they waited for the caretaker to open the gate to Buddy's pen. The caretaker carefully placed Buddy in their arms and said, "Happy birthday! We call him Buddy, but you can call him any name you want." He then snapped a picture of the twins as they held Buddy for the very first time. He then handed the picture to Mom and Dad as a present for the twins' birthday. Kip and Kinzi gave the caretaker a great big hug and thanked him for their new pet and that they were going to keep the name Buddy, for he was truly going to be their buddy. They loved him from the first time they saw him, and Buddy loved them too.

It was a joyous ride home with Buddy licking their faces while the twins tried to hold him still in the car. They were laughing and giggling as Buddy tried his best to jump up front with Mom and Dad. Even Mom and Dad got tickled by the tiny red miniature weenie dog.

After reaching home, Buddy ran from one twin to the other, still thinking he really might be seeing double. He finally realized that his dream had come true. This was what he had wanted for a long time: a nice family with kids to play with.

That night, Mom and Dad watched as Kip and Kinzi placed Buddy in his warm and cozy doggy bed. The twins gave Buddy a great big kiss and a gentle pat on his tiny head. Seeing the love for Buddy on Kip's and Kinzi's faces, Mom and Dad knew that they had made the right decision in letting the twins get the tiny red miniature weenie dog. After getting Buddy all settled, Kip and Kinzi turned to Mom and Dad and said with grins, "Thanks, this is the best birthday present ever!" Buddy let out a little sigh, as if to say, "Good night. Thanks for my dream home, and for letting me see *double*!"

Buddy Finds the Way Home

It was Thanksgiving Day, so all the family gathered at Grandma and Grandpa's house for another great Thanksgiving dinner. Mom was busy helping Grandma in the kitchen, and Dad sat on the front porch with Grandpa discussing old times. The rest of the relatives would be arriving soon.

The twins, Kip and Kinzi, and Buddy—their tiny red miniature weenie dog, who was adopted from the local dog pound and given to the twins as a birthday present—were very happy to be in the country, running and playing outside in the cool autumn breeze. They had been to Grandma and Grandpa's house many times before and had lots of fun following the many trails that led into the woods. Today was no different as they wandered down the trail. Kip and Kinzi had to run to keep up with Buddy as he chased a rabbit into the woods. Farther and farther they went, yelling, "Come back, Buddy! Buddy, come back!"

Finally the twins stopped to catch their breath and rest a minute. Buddy gave up the chase on the rabbit and ran back to Kip and Kinzi when he heard their familiar voices calling his name. Kip and Kinzi were so glad to see Buddy as he raced back toward them.

"Let's head back to Grandma and Grandpa's house because Mom and Dad will be very worried about us," said Kip.

"It's probably time to eat our Thanksgiving dinner," said Kinzi.

As Kip and Kinzi looked around to head back to Grandma and Grandpa's house, nothing looked the same. They had gotten off the main trail and were now lost. Buddy watched as Kip and Kinzi began to cry out, "We're lost! We don't know which way to go!"

Kip tried to be brave and said, "Don't worry, Kinzi! We will find our way back."

Buddy licked Kinzi's face as tears rolled down her cheeks. Suddenly, Buddy knew it was up to him to get the twins back safely. He began to sniff the ground and looked back at Kip and Kinzi as if to say, "It's this way! Follow me!" The twins followed as Buddy led the way.

Before long, they were on the familiar trail they had been down many times before, and just up ahead was Grandma and Grandpa's house. As they came closer, they could smell the wonderful Thanksgiving dinner and heard Mom and Dad calling their names. Mom and Dad breathed a sigh of relief when they saw the twins and Buddy coming down the trail. The twins began to tell Mom and Dad all about being lost and how Buddy led them safely back home.

It was a great Thanksgiving dinner with everyone giving thanks for all their many blessings. Mom and Dad were especially thankful for the twins getting back safely and also very thankful for Buddy, who found the way home.

Buddy's First Christmas

Buddy, the tiny red miniature weenie dog had only been living with the twins, Kip and Kinzi, for just six months. He had been adopted by the twins from the local dog pound as a gift for their third birthday.

Life was great for Buddy, living with Kip and Kinzi. Mom and Dad had grown to love Buddy too. The weather had turned really cold, so the twins had put a bright-yellow sweater on Buddy. He didn't like it much at first, but when he noticed himself in the hall mirror, he thought, *Not a bad looking dog, all dressed up in this yellow sweater!* He decided it felt warm, and if Kip and Kinzi liked it on him, he did too.

Buddy heard Mom and Dad talking about a Christmas tree. He didn't even know what Christmas was, but early the next morning, the whole family drove out into the woods not far from home. Buddy watched as Dad took an ax out of the back of the pickup truck. Before long, the large green tree hit the ground, and everyone helped to load the tree onto the truck and headed back home.

The next thing Buddy knew, the big tree was in the living room with all kinds of decorations on it. What a beautiful Christmas tree it was! Then Buddy noticed that there were lots of boxes with bows placed under the tree. He soon found out that they were called presents. Kip and Kinzi would show Buddy a present, and say, "This one is for you, Buddy!"

Buddy knew that he had to have help in getting the twins a Christmas present. He would go over to Mom as she sat in her favorite chair and then run back and forth to the Christmas tree. Mom seemed to sense what Buddy was trying to say. She patted Buddy on his tiny head and said, "Don't worry, Buddy, I'll help you find a present for Kip and Kinzi."

The next day, Mom showed Buddy a gift box, and inside was a picture of the twins and Buddy as the twins held him for the very first time when they had adopted him from the dog pound. *What a great gift*, Buddy thought. He knew that Kip and Kinzi would love it too. Buddy licked Mom's hand as if to say, "Thank you for this great gift!"

Christmas morning came, and it was a Christmas to remember! Everyone got great presents! Buddy even got a new leash, doggy treats, and another warm sweater. The best gift of all was when the twins opened the present that Buddy had given them. Mom had written on the box "To Kip and Kinzi, from Buddy." With tears in their eyes, they reached down and gave Buddy a great big hug and said, "Thank you, Buddy, for such a wonderful present!" Buddy now knew what Christmas was all about: *love, family,* and *giving!*

Buddy Saves the Day

It was the morning of the Annual Bake Sale to raise money for the local orphanage in Kip and Kinzi's hometown. Mom, who was chairman of the fund-raiser, got up early to begin her day. Kip and Kinzi, the twins, went along with Mom to help her set up tables in front of the bank for all the great-looking cakes and pies. Buddy, their tiny red miniature weenie dog, who was adopted from the local dog pound and given to them for their third birthday, was so glad that Mom let him go along too.

The twins held up signs as they walked up and down the sidewalk that read Bake Sale. Buddy was right at their heels, walking proudly behind them. They knew that the money raised was for a good cause. It was to help all the needy children at the orphanage.

Lots of people stopped by and bought a cake or a pie, or just gave a cash donation to help out. The bank was very busy that day, and lots of people gave large sums of money to help the orphanage. By midafternoon, the bank closed, and all the cakes and pies were gone and the money bag was full.

Mom decided to count the money collected and was pleasantly surprised by the large sum of money raised for the local orphanage. As Mom, Kip, and Kinzi began to clean up and take the tables to the car, Buddy noticed a strange-looking man coming down the sidewalk. He was walking hurriedly toward Mom's van. Mom had laid the money bag on the front seat of her van while she cleaned up from the bake sale. As the man got closer, Buddy watched as the man went to driver's side of Mom's van and opened the door. The man grabbed the money bag and began walking fast down the sidewalk. Mom yelled, "Bring that back!"

Buddy knew something was wrong by the fear in Mom's voice and seeing the strange man with the money bag. He ran quickly and grabbed the man by his pants leg, growling and barking, and then biting the man on the leg. The man began kicking and tried to get Buddy to release his pants leg, but Buddy would not let go. By this time, the bank guard heard the excitement and sounded an alarm. Soon police cars were everywhere! Buddy was still hanging on the man's pants leg when the police arrived.

The orphanage received the large donation from the bake sale and wanted to personally thank Buddy for helping to get the money back. They invited Kip, Kinzi, and Buddy to come spend the day with the children at the orphanage.

When the twins and Buddy arrived at the orphanage, there was a huge banner that read Buddy Saved the Day! Buddy couldn't read, but he just knew he had done something good as all the children began to gather around him and shout "Hooray for Buddy! Buddy saved the day!"

Buddy Goes Fishing

Spring had come, and it was time for the yearly family vacation. Each year Mom, Dad, and the twins, Kip and Kinzi, would spend the day at the lake near their home and fry all the fish that they caught for their supper. Of course, Buddy, their miniature weenie dog, had to go too. He went just about everywhere the family went since he was adopted from the local dog pound and given to the twins for their third birthday. This would be Buddy's first fishing trip with the family.

When they reached the lake, Buddy watched as Dad launched the big red fishing boat into the water. Buddy was very excited as Kip and Kinzi helped him into the boat. Mom and Dad were already seated as they waited for Kip and Kinzi to put on their life jackets. They even had a life jacket for Buddy.

The boat started, and off they went across the great big lake with the wind blowing in their faces. Buddy's ears were standing straight up. The twins had to laugh when they saw how funny Buddy looked. *This feels good!* thought Buddy, *but where's the fish?*

The boat finally came to a stop, and Mom, Dad, and the twins began to throw out their fishing lines. Time went by, but no one was catching a fish. It was getting late, and they were about to give up.

All of a sudden, Kip yelled, "I have a bite!" He began to reel in his fishing line, and you could see the big fish as it jumped back and forth in the water.

Everyone was so excited to see the big fish on Kip's line. Buddy was watching every move that the fish made. Kip gave a sigh of relief as he got the fish into the boat, but the fish jumped, and back into the water it went! The fishing line broke just as Buddy dove out of the boat and grabbed the fish by the tail. It went *splish-splash,* with Buddy trying hard to hold on to the fish. The fish was swinging Buddy from one side to the other.

Quick as a flash, Dad grabbed the fish net and scooped both Buddy and the fish up. Dad reached into the net and rescued Buddy and handed him to Kip and Kinzi. The twins were so glad that Buddy was all right. Buddy was also very happy to be back safe in the boat.

As the family headed to their fishing camp, Mom and Dad were very impressed with the brave little fishing dog. They knew that they would have fish for supper that night.

Back at the camp, Buddy watched as Mom fried the big fish for their supper. Kip and Kinzi were dancing around with excitement, calling Buddy their special fishing dog. Buddy enjoyed all the attention from the family, but thought to himself, *There must be an easier way to catch a fish.*

Buddy Becomes a Fireman

The big carnival and parade in Kip and Kinzi's hometown started today. The twins had ridden on the fire truck many times, but today was a little different. Today, they had Buddy, their miniature weenie dog, with them. Buddy had been adopted from the local dog pound and given to them as a special present for their third birthday. This would be Buddy's first ride on the great big fire truck.

As Kip, Kinzi, and Buddy climbed onto the big red fire truck, the fire chief was explaining to all the kids how a fireman helps so many people save their homes from a total disaster caused by fires. Kip, Kinzi, and Buddy had seen firemen on TV fighting fires and saving many lives. Little did they know, they would face such a situation that very day.

That afternoon, Kip and Kinzi and Buddy were playing in their backyard with their Slip 'N Slide. The twins laughed as Buddy grabbed the long black water hose and tried to run with it.

Mr. Kimble, their neighbor, waved to the twins and Buddy as he went out in his backyard to burn his garbage. After a few minutes, Mr. Kimble got into his car and drove away. Before long, Kip, Kinzi, and Buddy smelled the smoke from Mr. Kimble's garbage and watched as the fire seemed to get bigger and bigger. The wind had started blowing, and you could see tiny pieces of garbage flying through the air.

The twins continued to play with their Slip 'N Slide and laughed as Buddy ran back and forth through the water. By this time, Buddy was soaked, as well as the twins.

Just as the twins were about to take another run down the Slip 'N Slide, Buddy began to bark and run back and forth to Mr. Kimble's fence. Buddy kept barking and looking at Kip and Kinzi with each bark. The twins were puzzled as it seemed Buddy was trying to tell them something. Buddy then grabbed the long hose, ran to the fence, and put the hose down just where the fire had started to come under the fence. Buddy then grabbed the wet Slip 'N Slide and dragged it to the fence.

By this time, Mom and Dad had run outside when they heard Buddy barking excitedly to see what was going on. The twins saw the fire and started yelling, "Fire! Fire!" Dad ran quickly and called the fire department. Soon sirens began to sound as the big red fire truck came down the street and pulled into Mr. Kimble's drive.

The firemen were able to put the fire out before it did much damage thanks to Buddy, who noticed the fire and pulled the water hose and Slip 'N Slide over to the fence to stop it from spreading.

Mr. Kimble came driving up, just as the firemen were about to drive away. "What happened?" he asked. The firemen explained to Mr. Kimble about his garbage getting out and how Buddy kept it from spreading.

Mr. Kimble was very thankful to Buddy and the firemen for putting the fire out. Buddy felt so proud as the fire chief and Mr. Kimble bragged about him. Kip and Kinzi were very proud of Buddy too. The fire chief placed a small red hat on Buddy's head and said with a loud voice, "Buddy is now an honorary fireman!"

Buddy's First Birthday

It had been nearly a year since Buddy, the tiny red miniature weenie dog, came to live with Kip and Kinzi, the twins. He had been adopted from the local dog pound and given to the twins for their third birthday. Every day was a new day of adventure for them. The twins would turn four in just a few days, and a huge birthday party was planned for them. All the neighborhood kids, aunts, uncles, grandmas, and grandpas would be there at the city park for the big day. And of course, Buddy would be there too. Buddy was their favorite birthday present from last year.

Buddy seemed to sense the excitement and started thinking what he could get for the twins for their fourth birthday. Dogs don't have money to go to the store to buy things, so he would have to come up with something on his own.

Kip and Kinzi told Mom and Dad that they wanted to share their birthday with Buddy. They didn't know exactly what day Buddy was born, but they knew he had been with them since their last birthday when they got him from the dog pound and he was just a pup, so he had to be about a year old now.

The twins asked Mom and Dad if Buddy could have a few of his doggy friends at the party. Several of the neighborhood kids had brought their dogs over to meet Buddy when they came over to play. Mom and Dad agreed to let Buddy and his doggy friends come to the big birthday party as long as the dogs were kept on a leash. So the word was out! Saturday's big birthday party was not only for Kip and Kinzi but for Buddy too.

When Saturday finally came, the city park was decorated with huge, bright red, yellow, blue, and green balloons, with ribbons flying in the air. Party hats were placed on all the kids' heads as well as their dogs' heads. It looked like a carnival with a dog show!

It was a great birthday party for Kip and Kinzi as well as for Buddy. Kip and Kinzi got lots of great presents, and Buddy did too. Kip and Kinzi had given Buddy a doggy pillow with *I love you, Buddy* written on it. Buddy had tears in his eyes as he ran under the table, and out he came with two flowers that he had picked for the twins. They gave him a big hug and said, "Thanks for the beautiful flowers."

As all the kids began to gather around and sing "Happy Birthday" to Kip and Kinzi, all the dogs joined in with loud barking. What a birthday to remember! There were cake and punch for everyone, even Buddy's doggy friends. Buddy knew that this had to be the very best *first birthday* any dog could ever have!

Buddy Goes to School

It was the day before school started. Kip, Kinzi, and Buddy were very excited as they looked at all the new school clothes, backpacks, and school supplies lying on the bed. Buddy grabbed a bright-red shirt and started running with it. Kip caught him just before he ran under the bed. "No, Buddy!" yelled Kip and Kinzi as they fussed at him, trying to hold back a grin.

Buddy, the tiny red miniature weenie dog, had been with Kip and Kinzi, the twins, since he was just a pup. He was adopted by them from the local dog pound as a present for their third birthday. Buddy was still very tiny and still looked like a tiny hotdog. He had spent every day with the twins for as long as he could remember. Kip and Kinzi were very special to him. They did everything together. Not a day went by that Buddy was not at their side. Now the twins were old enough to start school. Tomorrow was the big day! *What about me?* thought Buddy. *What will I do all day without the twins to play with?*

That night Buddy slept next to the backpacks left by the front door. The backpacks were all ready for school the next day. It was chilly during the night, so Buddy snuggled inside Kinzi's backpack and slept all warm and cozy.

School morning came. Kip and Kinzi bounced out of bed, ate their breakfast, dressed for school, and grabbed their backpacks, and out the door they went to catch the big yellow school bus that stopped in front of their house.

With tears in her eyes, Mom waved bye as she watched the big yellow school bus pull away. *This will be a lonely day for me and Buddy,* she thought.

In all the excitement, Mom and the twins had forgotten all about Buddy. Where was he? Mom called his name again and again as she went from room to room. Where could Buddy be? The twins would be very upset if Buddy did not show up by the time they got home from school. Mom opened the front door, still calling Buddy's name over and over. There was no sign of the tiny red miniature weenie dog anywhere.

Meanwhile, Kip and Kinzi stepped off the school bus and hurried to their classroom. The bell sounded, and Buddy let out a little howl. The bell was so loud that nobody seemed to hear the tiny red miniature weenie dog inside Kinzi's backpack.

The teacher welcomed each student to the classroom and asked them to get out their pencil and paper. As Kinzi reached inside her backpack to get her pencil, she felt something soft and warm. She looked down, and there sat Buddy, staring up at her with his tiny brown eyes. Kinzi whispered to Kip, "Buddy is inside my backpack."

Kip whispered back, "Don't let the teacher see him, or we will be in trouble!"

The teacher heard the whispers and asked, "Is there a problem?"

Kip and Kinzi shook their heads and answered at the same time, "No, Ma'am."

Buddy was quiet as a mouse as he stayed inside the backpack. Kinzi asked the teacher if she could please take her backpack out during recess. The teacher looked puzzled but said, "I guess so." Buddy was so small that he ran out of the backpack and under the merry-go-round without anyone seeing him. When recess was over, Buddy ran back inside Kinzi's backpack and took a nap.

Lunchtime came, with Kip and Kinzi dropping a portion of their sandwich into the backpack for Buddy. Buddy thought to himself, *School's not so bad. I might come back again tomorrow!*

Buddy had been very quiet until the school bell rang to go home. Suddenly, he let out another little howl. The teacher quickly turned around and asked, "Who was that?"

Kip and Kinzi hurried out the door to catch their bus, saying softly, "No, Buddy!"

Buddy stayed hidden in the backpack on the bus ride home. As soon as they reached the front door, Buddy jumped out of the backpack and started running, jumping, and barking. He was very tired of being stuffed inside the backpack for most of the day.

Mom opened the door to see Kip and Kinzi playing with Buddy. She asked "How was school today?" and "Where have you been, Buddy?"

Kip and Kinzi smiled and said "School was great!" as they dropped their backpacks on the floor and began to tell Mom all about their day.

Buddy looked guilty as he heard the twins telling Mom all about him getting into Kinzi's backpack and going to school with them.

Mom laughed as she listened to the story and told the twins how she had been looking for Buddy all day.

Buddy spotted the backpacks lying on the floor and quietly tried to sneak inside Kinzi's backpack once again. The twins saw him and shouted, "No Buddy. No more school for you!"

Buddy Goes to the Zoo

It was a bright and sunny Saturday morning as Kip, Kinzi, Mom, Dad, and Buddy, their tiny miniature weenie dog, headed to the zoo. Mom and Dad had promised to take the twins to the zoo if they made good grades at school. Kip and Kinzi begged Mom and Dad to let Buddy go too. He was adopted from the local dog pound as a present for the twins' third birthday and stayed close by their side. So off the family went with a picnic basket and Buddy safely secured on a leash.

First stop was the lion's cage. *What a big kitty cat,* thought Buddy. The lion let out a loud roar, and Buddy jumped back, wondering, *What happened to the cat's meow?* Kip and Kinzi laughed as they led Buddy on to see the other animals.

They came to the bears' cage, and the bears growled noisily at Buddy. Buddy looked puzzled, thinking the twins' stuffed bear never made that kind of noise. He was sure glad because he liked to lie down beside the bear on their bed and take a nap.

Next were the giraffes. *What a long neck they have, and look at all the spots!* Buddy tried to stretch his neck like the giraffe's but had no luck.

Things were going great until Buddy noticed a kangaroo. The baby kangaroo was inside the mama kangaroo's pouch. *What a fun ride that would be,* thought Buddy. Suddenly, Buddy jerked the leash out of Kip's hand, ran under the fence, and jumped inside the kangaroo's pouch. You could see his tiny head and ears sticking up next to the baby kangaroo.

The mama kangaroo didn't seem to notice the tiny red miniature weenie dog inside her pouch.

The crowd gathered around as everyone watched to see what would happen next. Kip and Kinzi were so worried that Buddy would be hurt. Mom and Dad called the zoo attendant and told him about Buddy being in the kangaroo's pouch. By this time, all the children and parents were pointing to the kangaroo with the tiny red miniature weenie dog in its pouch.

The zoo attendant entered the pen and reached out to get Buddy, but the kangaroo hopped away before he could reach him. *This is a fun ride,* thought Buddy. After a few more hops, Buddy began to feel dizzy. *Where is my family? I want out of here!*

As the kangaroo hopped next to the fence, the twins shouted, "Here, Buddy!" When Buddy heard their familiar voices, he jumped out of the kangaroo pouch and ran as fast as his tiny legs could go, straight back to Kip and Kinzi. The crowd began to clap and yell with relief.

What was all the excitement? thought Buddy. *That sure was a strange backpack that kangaroo had!* Buddy decided that he liked Kip and Kinzi's backpack much more then the kangaroo's. Kip and Kinzi were so happy to see Buddy all safe and sound. Mom and Dad even gave Buddy a gentle pat on the head.

What a day of adventure the family had at the zoo! As the family walked back to car, Buddy wagged his tail and let out a little howl as if to say, "Wonder what we will do next Saturday?"

Buddy Becomes a Paperboy

For many years now, Kip and Kinzi would wait impatiently each morning as Dad read the morning paper. He would then give it to the twins, who would read the comics and work on the crossword puzzles before they headed off to school. This morning, as Kip and Kinzi came down the stairs, they noticed that Dad was not reading the paper as he usually did. That seemed odd, so the twins wanted to know why. Dad explained that the paper was missing. He was pretty sure that he had paid the bill, and the paperboy was always on time.

Kip and Kinzi noticed Buddy, their miniature weenie dog who had been adopted from the local dog pound as a birthday gift, looking strangely sad when Dad mentioned the missing paper. Buddy had never bothered the newspaper before, so Kip and Kinzi were sure hoping that he had not destroyed Dad's morning paper. They knew Dad would be very upset, and they also missed the comics and crossword puzzles. Hopefully, the paper would be there the next morning.

Next morning came, and still no paper. Kip and Kinzi again noticed that Buddy seemed to hover in the corner with a strange look on his face when the missing paper was mentioned.

After three days and still no paper, Dad decided to call the newspaper office to check on his subscription to the newspaper. They told him that his bill was paid and that his newspaper was being delivered every single morning. Dad looked confused and just shook his head.

Kip and Kinzi decided that they had to find out about the missing paper. It had been several days now, and the paper was still not outside on the front sidewalk as it had been for as long as they could remember.

That night, before going to bed, the twins set their alarm clock for four the next morning. That way, they would be up early to see if the paperboy was really bringing their newspaper.

When the alarm went off the next morning, Kip and Kinzi got up quietly and went down the stairs to sit by the front door and wait for the paperboy. They dozed off for a minute, but suddenly, they heard the newspaper hit the sidewalk in front of their house. They jumped to their feet and ran out to pick up the paper. Just as they reached down to pick up the paper, something very small grabbed the paper and started running down the street with it. Kip and Kinzi started running after the paper as it was being dragged down the sidewalk by some small something! Just then, they saw Buddy, their miniature weenie dog, run through the doggy door of Mr. Miller's house with the morning paper in his mouth.

The twins could not understand why Buddy would do such a thing. They stood there in disbelief, as they watched Buddy come back out the doggy door without the paper. Kip and Kinzi began to fuss at Buddy for stealing Dad's paper, still wondering why Buddy took the paper into Mr. Miller's house.

The twins knew that they had to tell Dad about Buddy stealing his newspaper. They hoped that Dad would not be so mad that he would want to give Buddy away.

By the time the twins got back to their front door, Mom and Dad were up drinking coffee. Kip and Kinzi told Mom and Dad all about seeing Buddy stealing the newspaper and going into Mr. Miller's house. Mom and Dad began to scold the twins for going out without telling them and how dangerous it could have been. Kip and Kinzi thought, *This is strange. We're the ones in trouble, but Buddy is the thief. Mom and Dad had not fussed at Buddy at all.*

The twins soon found out why. Dad told them that Mr. Miller had been very sick and had to stay in bed for several weeks. Buddy knew that there was something wrong because Mr. Miller always took a morning walk. Mr. Miller would stop and pet Buddy on the head and give him a doggy treat before picking up his morning paper.

Mr. Miller's dog, Zip, had died a few weeks before Mr. Miller got sick. It was very sad for Mr. Miller and for Buddy too. Zip had also been a good friend to Buddy. Mr. Miller decided to cancel his newspaper since he didn't have Zip to bring the paper to his bed while he was sick.

Buddy heard the neighbors talking about Mr. Miller being so sick. Buddy decided that he wanted to do something nice for Mr. Miller so that's why he took the newspaper to him each morning. Neither Mom and Dad, nor Kip and Kinzi could be mad at Buddy for trying to help Mr. Miller. They were actually very proud of him for caring for a neighbor.

Mom and Dad decided to pay for Mr. Miller's newspaper subscription for they knew that Buddy would make sure that Mr. Miller got his newspaper. Mr. Miller was very grateful to Mom and Dad as well as to his *special paperboy*, Buddy.

The family was so glad that things were back to normal and that the mystery of the missing newspaper had been solved. Buddy had a proud look on his face as he wondered to himself, *And I thought newspapers were just for chewing up!*

Printed in the United States
by Baker & Taylor Publisher Services